I Can Draw...
Wild Animals

Artwork by Terry Longhurst

Text by Amanda O'Neill

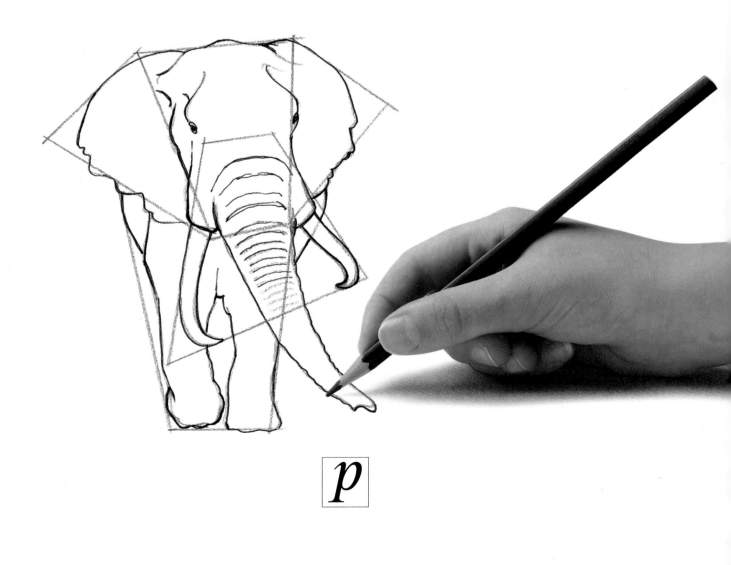

p

This is a Parragon Book
This edition published in 2002

Parragon
Queen Street House
4 Queen Street
Bath BA1 1HE, UK

Designed, packaged, and produced by
Touchstone

ISBN 0-75257-032-3

Artwork by Terry Longhurst
Text by Amanda O'Neill
Edited by Philip de Ste. Croix

Printed in Dubai, U.A.E

About this book

Everybody can enjoy drawing, but sometimes it's hard to know where to begin. The subject you want to draw can look very complicated. This book shows you how to start, by breaking down your subject into a series of simple shapes.

The tools you need are very simple. The basic requirements are paper and pencils. Very thin paper wears through if you have to rub out a line, so choose paper that is thick enough to work on. Pencils come with different leads, from very hard to very soft. Very hard pencils give a clean, thin line which is best for finishing drawings. Very soft ones give a thicker, darker line. You will probably find a medium pencil most useful.

If you want to colour in your drawing, you have the choice of paints, coloured inks, or felt-tip pens. Fine felt-tips are useful for drawing outlines, thick felt-tips are better for colouring in.

The most important tool you have is your own eyes. The mistake many people make is to draw what they think something looks like, instead of really looking at it carefully first. Half the secret of making your drawing look good is getting the proportions right. Study your subject before you start, and break it down in your mind into sections. Check how much bigger, or longer, or shorter, one part is than another. Notice where one part joins another, and at what angle. See where there are flowing curves, and where there are straight lines.

The step-by-step drawings in this book show you exactly how to do this. Each subject is broken down into easy stages, so you can build up your drawing one piece at a time. Look carefully at each shape before – and after – you draw it. If you find you have drawn it the wrong size or in the wrong place, correct it before you go on. Then the next shape will fit into place, and piece-by-piece you can build up a fantastic picture.

Tiger

The tiger is a large and powerful predator which usually hunts by stealth at night. It feeds mainly on wild oxen and buffalo which it kills with a bite to the back of the neck or the throat. Tigers are found in south and south-east Asia.

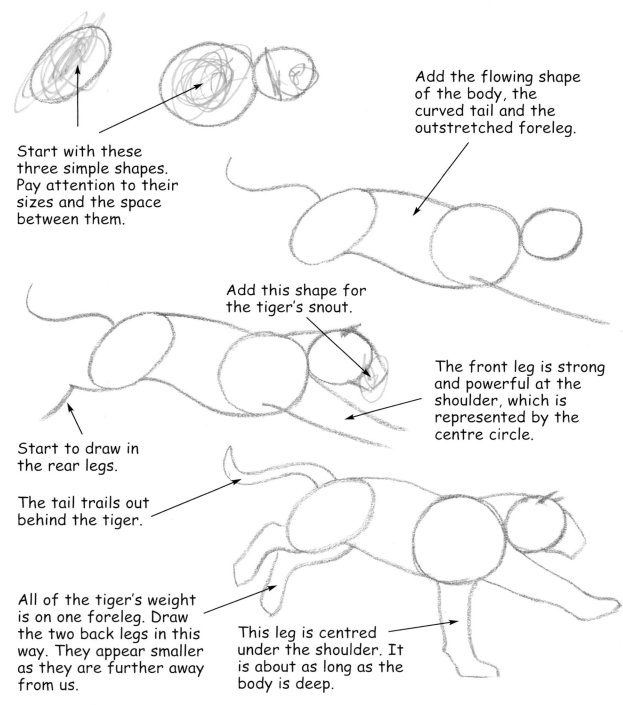

Start with these three simple shapes. Pay attention to their sizes and the space between them.

Add the flowing shape of the body, the curved tail and the outstretched foreleg.

Add this shape for the tiger's snout.

The front leg is strong and powerful at the shoulder, which is represented by the centre circle.

Start to draw in the rear legs.

The tail trails out behind the tiger.

All of the tiger's weight is on one foreleg. Draw the two back legs in this way. They appear smaller as they are further away from us.

This leg is centred under the shoulder. It is about as long as the body is deep.

Begin to add details for the eyes, mouth and the striped coat.

The underside is paler than the back, and without stripes.

The nose, mouth and eye bring the head to life.

Begin to define the tiger's shape with ink.

The dark stripes break up the tiger's solid outline.

The strong colours of the tiger's coat, its stripes and paler underside are valuable camouflage when it hides in long grass, patiently stalking its prey.

White Rhino

The rhino is a vegetarian – but it is also one of Africa's most dangerous animals. It is built like a tank, and armed with sharp horns. A charging rhino can knock an elephant down! The White Rhino is less aggressive than its cousin, the Black Rhino, and is normally gentle unless disturbed.

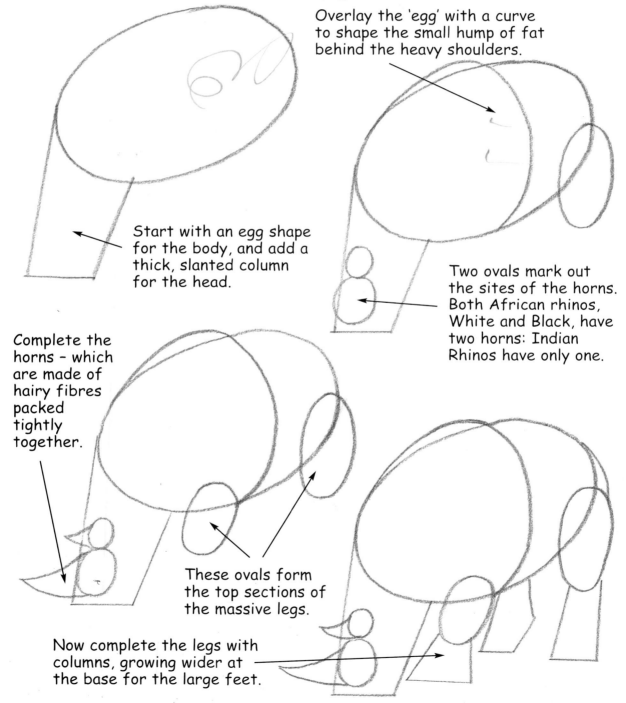

Overlay the 'egg' with a curve to shape the small hump of fat behind the heavy shoulders.

Start with an egg shape for the body, and add a thick, slanted column for the head.

Two ovals mark out the sites of the horns. Both African rhinos, White and Black, have two horns: Indian Rhinos have only one.

Complete the horns – which are made of hairy fibres packed tightly together.

These ovals form the top sections of the massive legs.

Now complete the legs with columns, growing wider at the base for the large feet.

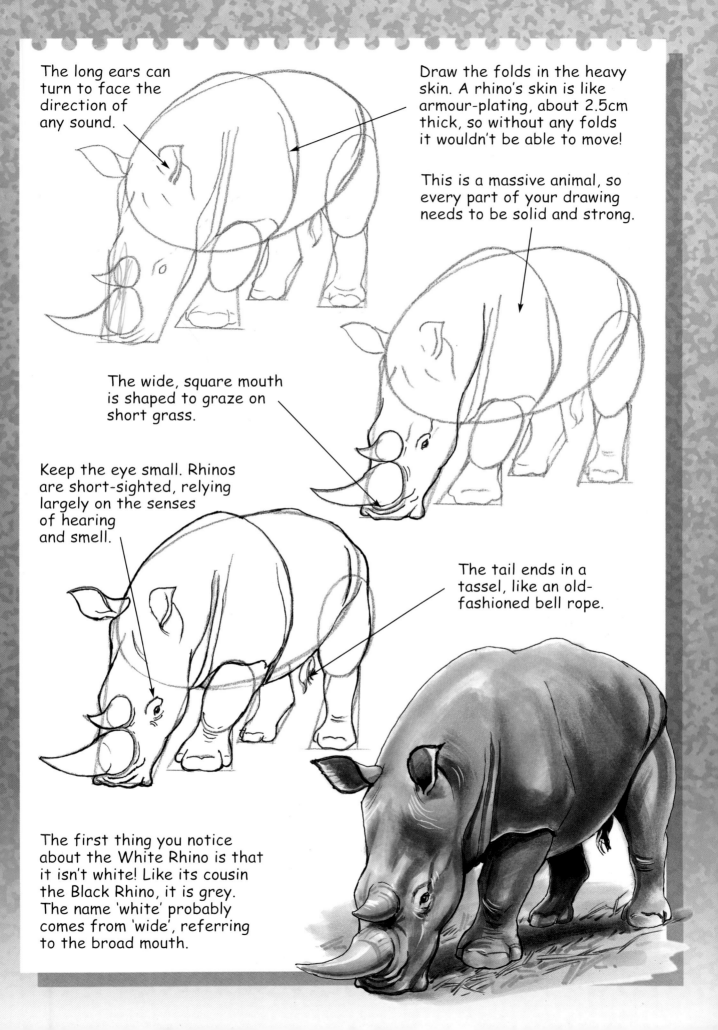

The long ears can turn to face the direction of any sound.

Draw the folds in the heavy skin. A rhino's skin is like armour-plating, about 2.5cm thick, so without any folds it wouldn't be able to move!

This is a massive animal, so every part of your drawing needs to be solid and strong.

The wide, square mouth is shaped to graze on short grass.

Keep the eye small. Rhinos are short-sighted, relying largely on the senses of hearing and smell.

The tail ends in a tassel, like an old-fashioned bell rope.

The first thing you notice about the White Rhino is that it isn't white! Like its cousin the Black Rhino, it is grey. The name 'white' probably comes from 'wide', referring to the broad mouth.

Scarlet Macaw

Macaws are the biggest and brightest-coloured members of the parrot family. They live in the tropical rain-forests of Central and South America. They are superb fliers, and equally good at climbing through the trees where they live.

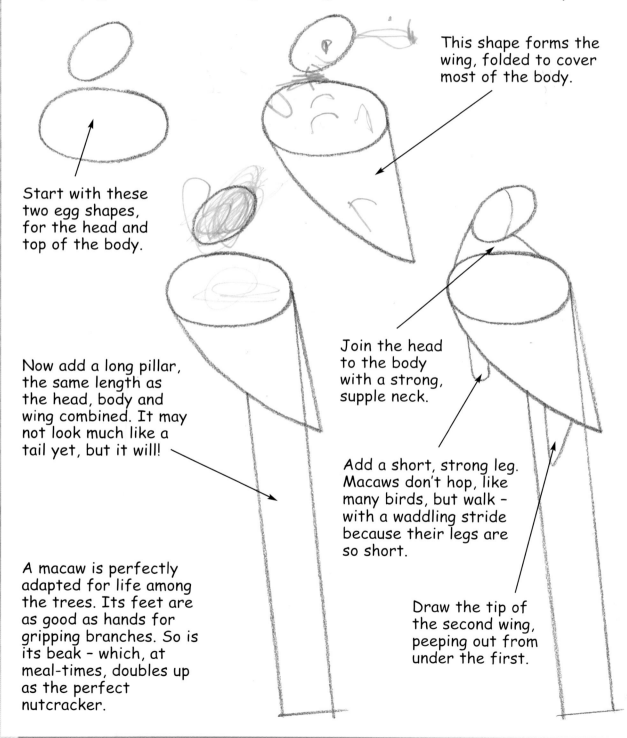

Start with these two egg shapes, for the head and top of the body.

This shape forms the wing, folded to cover most of the body.

Now add a long pillar, the same length as the head, body and wing combined. It may not look much like a tail yet, but it will!

Join the head to the body with a strong, supple neck.

Add a short, strong leg. Macaws don't hop, like many birds, but walk – with a waddling stride because their legs are so short.

A macaw is perfectly adapted for life among the trees. Its feet are as good as hands for gripping branches. So is its beak – which, at meal-times, doubles up as the perfect nutcracker.

Draw the tip of the second wing, peeping out from under the first.

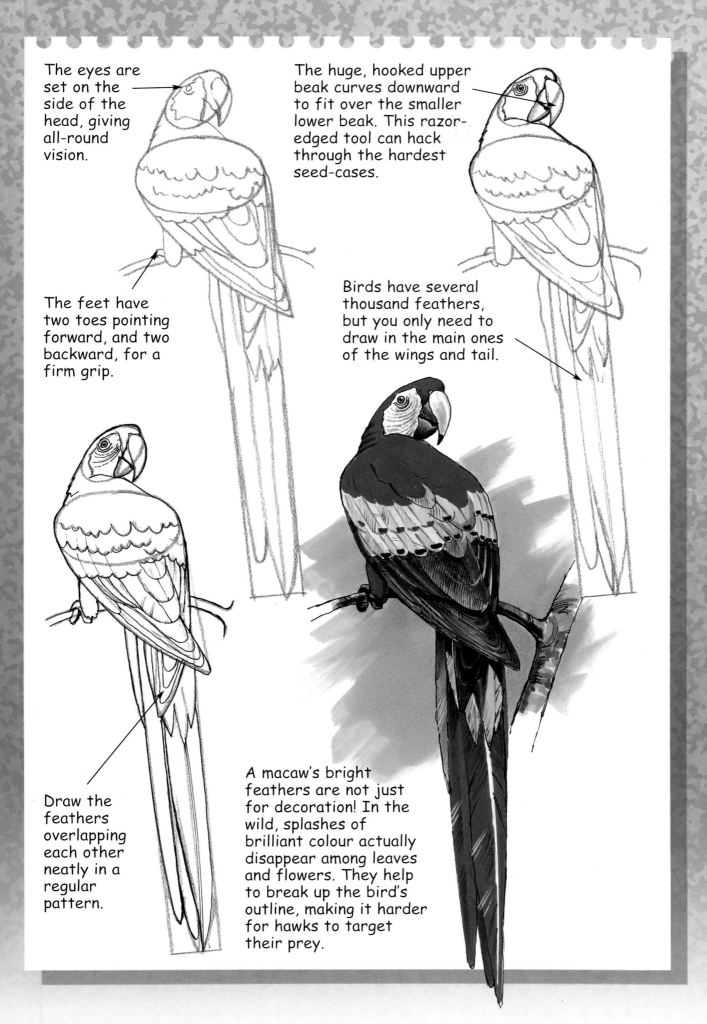

The eyes are set on the side of the head, giving all-round vision.

The huge, hooked upper beak curves downward to fit over the smaller lower beak. This razor-edged tool can hack through the hardest seed-cases.

The feet have two toes pointing forward, and two backward, for a firm grip.

Birds have several thousand feathers, but you only need to draw in the main ones of the wings and tail.

Draw the feathers overlapping each other neatly in a regular pattern.

A macaw's bright feathers are not just for decoration! In the wild, splashes of brilliant colour actually disappear among leaves and flowers. They help to break up the bird's outline, making it harder for hawks to target their prey.

Crocodile

Crocodiles belong to an ancient family, dating back to the time of the dinosaurs. They live mostly in tropical rivers and lakes and are beautifully adapted to a life in the water, although they also like to bask in the sun on shore.

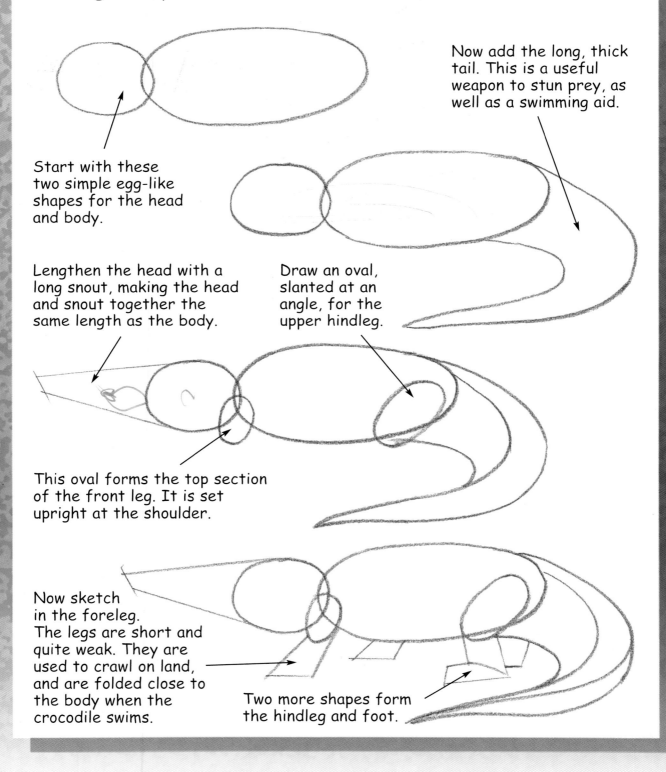

Now add the long, thick tail. This is a useful weapon to stun prey, as well as a swimming aid.

Start with these two simple egg-like shapes for the head and body.

Lengthen the head with a long snout, making the head and snout together the same length as the body.

Draw an oval, slanted at an angle, for the upper hindleg.

This oval forms the top section of the front leg. It is set upright at the shoulder.

Now sketch in the foreleg. The legs are short and quite weak. They are used to crawl on land, and are folded close to the body when the crocodile swims.

Two more shapes form the hindleg and foot.

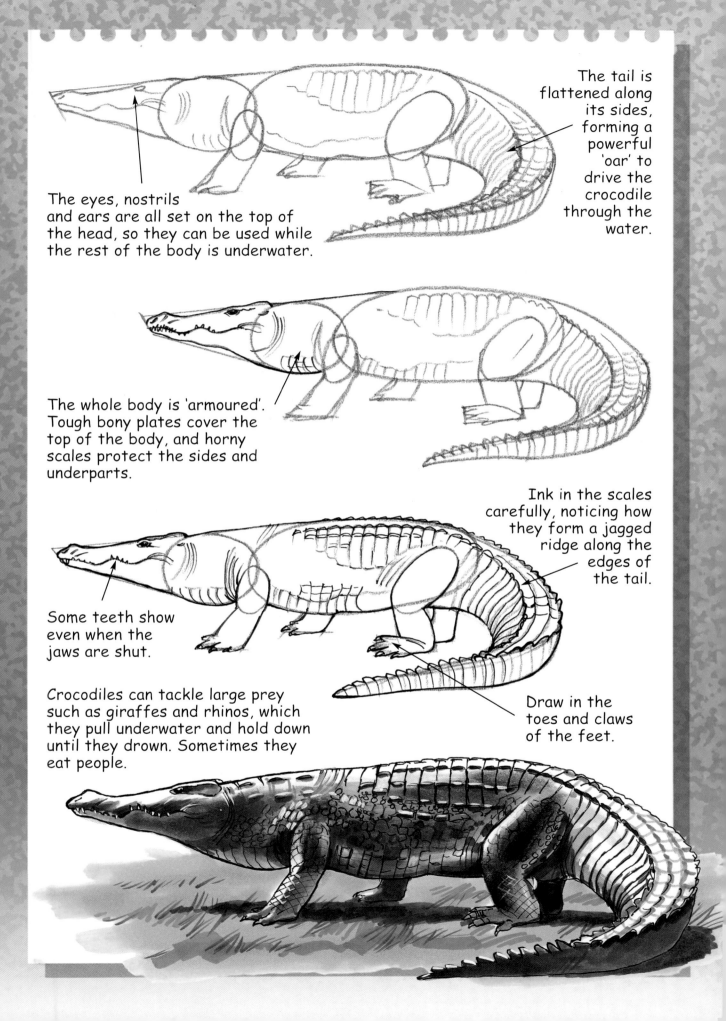

The tail is flattened along its sides, forming a powerful 'oar' to drive the crocodile through the water.

The eyes, nostrils and ears are all set on the top of the head, so they can be used while the rest of the body is underwater.

The whole body is 'armoured'. Tough bony plates cover the top of the body, and horny scales protect the sides and underparts.

Ink in the scales carefully, noticing how they form a jagged ridge along the edges of the tail.

Some teeth show even when the jaws are shut.

Crocodiles can tackle large prey such as giraffes and rhinos, which they pull underwater and hold down until they drown. Sometimes they eat people.

Draw in the toes and claws of the feet.

Gorilla

Gorillas are the biggest and heaviest of the apes. In the forests of tropical Africa, they live in family groups headed by big males, who develop silver backs with age. These gentle giants feed on leaves and shoots, but are too heavy to climb trees.

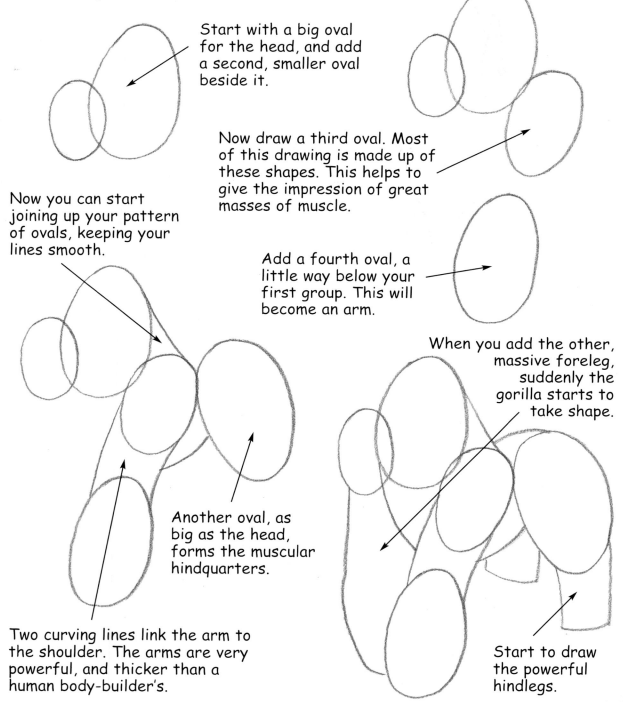

Start with a big oval for the head, and add a second, smaller oval beside it.

Now draw a third oval. Most of this drawing is made up of these shapes. This helps to give the impression of great masses of muscle.

Now you can start joining up your pattern of ovals, keeping your lines smooth.

Add a fourth oval, a little way below your first group. This will become an arm.

When you add the other, massive foreleg, suddenly the gorilla starts to take shape.

Another oval, as big as the head, forms the muscular hindquarters.

Two curving lines link the arm to the shoulder. The arms are very powerful, and thicker than a human body-builder's.

Start to draw the powerful hindlegs.

Now sketch in the face. Start in the centre, with the flattened nose, to help you to space the features. Note that the huge domed forehead takes up nearly half the space.

Start inking in your outlines, suggesting the shape of fur at the top of the head.

The arms are longer than a human's, but the legs are shorter. Make sure you have the proportions right before finishing off your drawing.

The gorilla stands with its fingers bent over, and its weight on its knuckles.

Gorillas have no home. They wander through the forest, stopping to feed. Every night they build fresh sleeping nests of branches, which they abandon next morning.

Meerkat

This little mongoose is found in the grasslands and deserts of southern Africa. It lives in large family groups, which work together to keep family members fed and safe. Males take turns at sentry duty. Standing upright on a tree or rock, they watch for danger.

This shape – like an egg flattened at the top – forms the long, narrow head with its pointed snout.

Copy this shape carefully. It forms guidelines for the upright body, all four legs and even the branch on which the Meerkat sentry perches.

Now add a neck, and draw a long sausage-shape for the body. Make sure this runs down the outline at the back, but leave a gap at the front and a larger one at the base.

Draw the first foreleg, hanging down. It is shaped very much like a human arm, with dangling hands.

This small shape will form the top of a hindleg. The legs are strong enough for the Meerkat to stand up erect for long periods.

Now follow the front edge of your guideline to mark out the far shoulder and second foreleg.

Two bold curving lines form the second hind leg. Finish it off with a long foot.

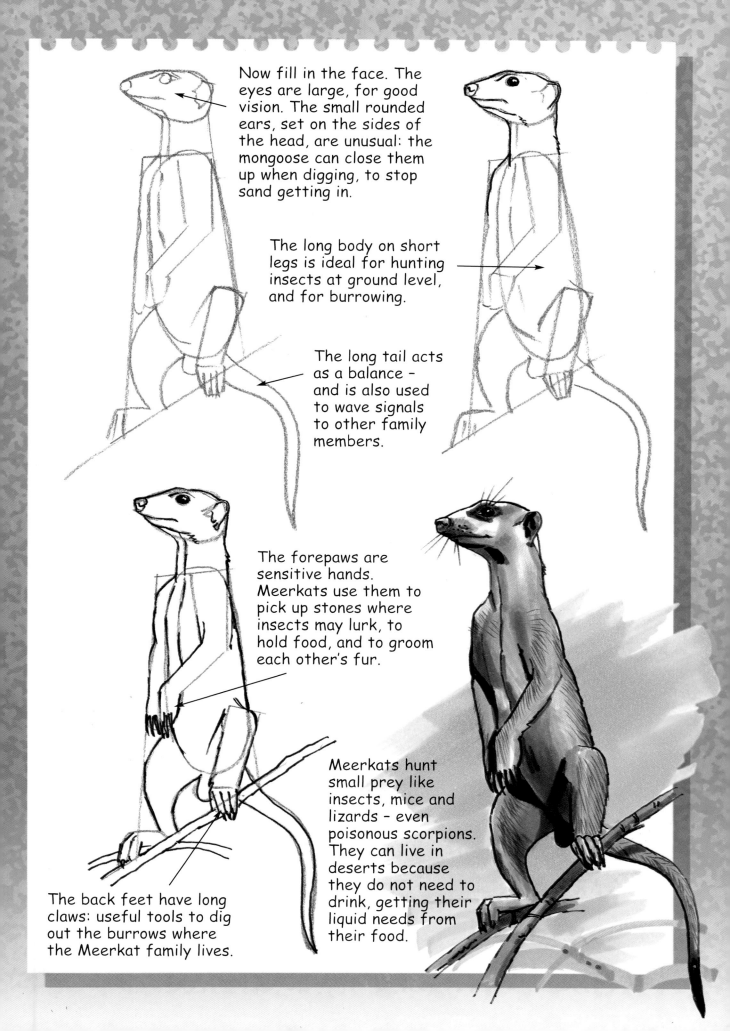

Now fill in the face. The eyes are large, for good vision. The small rounded ears, set on the sides of the head, are unusual: the mongoose can close them up when digging, to stop sand getting in.

The long body on short legs is ideal for hunting insects at ground level, and for burrowing.

The long tail acts as a balance – and is also used to wave signals to other family members.

The forepaws are sensitive hands. Meerkats use them to pick up stones where insects may lurk, to hold food, and to groom each other's fur.

Meerkats hunt small prey like insects, mice and lizards – even poisonous scorpions. They can live in deserts because they do not need to drink, getting their liquid needs from their food.

The back feet have long claws: useful tools to dig out the burrows where the Meerkat family lives.

Lion

This big, handsome cat is nicknamed 'King of Beasts' because he looks so noble. But really he is a lazy creature who lets his female lionesses do the hunting. Lions are the only cats to live in large family groups, called prides. They are found only in Africa, and in the Gir Forest of India.

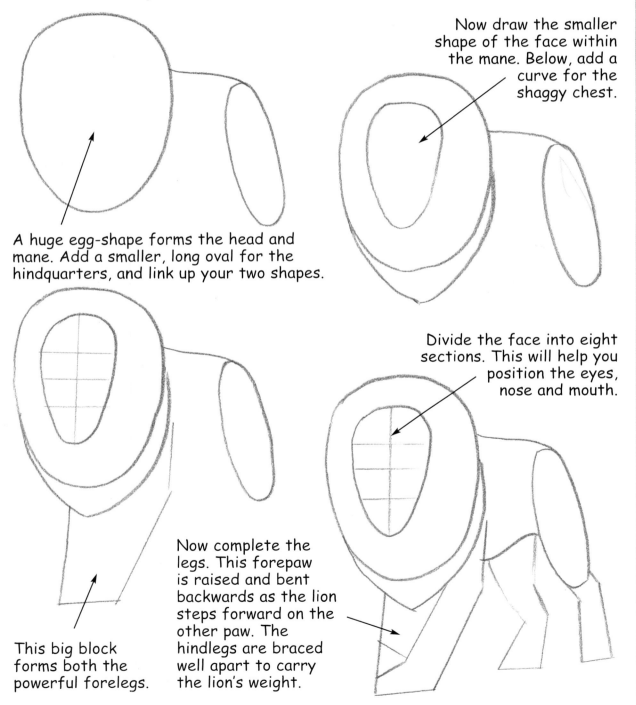

A huge egg-shape forms the head and mane. Add a smaller, long oval for the hindquarters, and link up your two shapes.

Now draw the smaller shape of the face within the mane. Below, add a curve for the shaggy chest.

Divide the face into eight sections. This will help you position the eyes, nose and mouth.

This big block forms both the powerful forelegs.

Now complete the legs. This forepaw is raised and bent backwards as the lion steps forward on the other paw. The hindlegs are braced well apart to carry the lion's weight.

Now use the guidelines you drew across the face to position the eyes, broad nose and open mouth. The rounded ears are hidden in the mane.

Most of the lion's coat is short, but add some shaggy hair hanging down under the chest, and a tassel at the end of the tail.

Only males have a mane, and it varies as much as human hair. It may be thick or thin, fair, dark or reddish, and some lions have no mane at all.

This is a big, powerful animal, weighing about as much as two men. The lioness is smaller and more lightly built.

The feet end in big, rounded toes. The claws are hidden in sheaths, like a house cat's, until they are needed.

The tawny colour of the lion's coat blends with dry grass and the soil. This camouflage is valuable when lions lie in wait for prey. Most prey species can outrun a lion, so these hunters prefer an ambush to a chase.

Giraffe

The Giraffe is the tallest living animal. In the African grasslands, it can feed on the scattered trees which other animals cannot reach.

Start with an oval for the surprisingly short body, and add guidelines for the long legs.

Draw two slanting lines for the long neck, taking care with the angles. The upper line is set roughly in the centre of the body shape, to form the sloping shoulders.

Cap the neck with a long low triangle for the head.

Start marking out the position of the legs with these simple lines. The legs are so long that, despite its long neck, a Giraffe has to spread its legs to reach the ground with its mouth.

Still using your guidelines, shape the neck and shoulders.

Draw the slender legs within the guidelines.

Sketch in the face, with ears, eyes and horns. Give a little droop to the lips.

Draw in the tops of the legs, where they join the body. Add a long, tasselled tail – the perfect flyswitch, essential in hot countries where flies are a constant nuisance.

A short, bristly mane runs all the way down the neck. Unlike a horse, however, the Giraffe has no forelock.

The horns are short and covered with fur. All Giraffes have at least two horns; some have three, and some have five.

Draw in the beautiful pattern of brown blotches on white. You don't need to copy this picture exactly: no two Giraffes have exactly the same pattern!

Giraffes are sociable animals. They live in family groups, which often gather together to form herds of as many as 70 animals.

South African Oryx

This large, handsome African antelope is a desert dweller. It sometimes goes without drinking, getting all the water it needs from plants. Its impressive horns can be more than a metre long, and are as straight as walking sticks. They are deadly weapons for defence, even against lions.

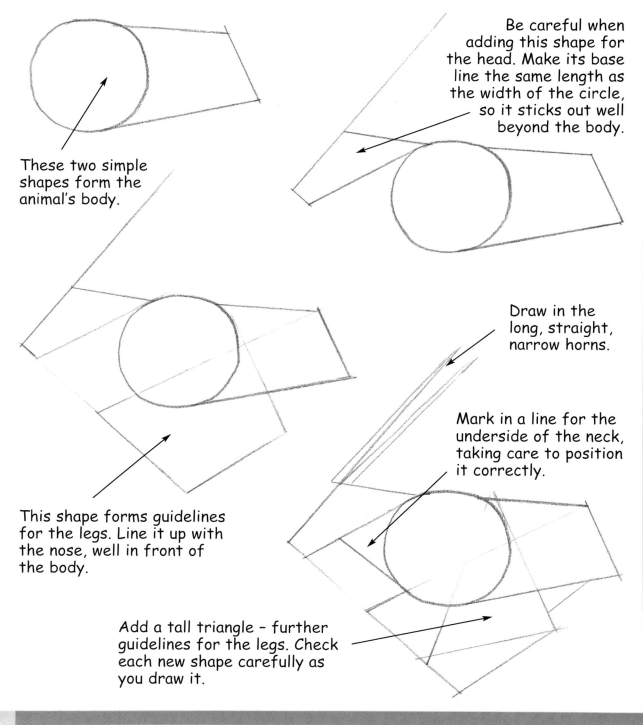

These two simple shapes form the animal's body.

Be careful when adding this shape for the head. Make its base line the same length as the width of the circle, so it sticks out well beyond the body.

Draw in the long, straight, narrow horns.

This shape forms guidelines for the legs. Line it up with the nose, well in front of the body.

Mark in a line for the underside of the neck, taking care to position it correctly.

Add a tall triangle – further guidelines for the legs. Check each new shape carefully as you draw it.

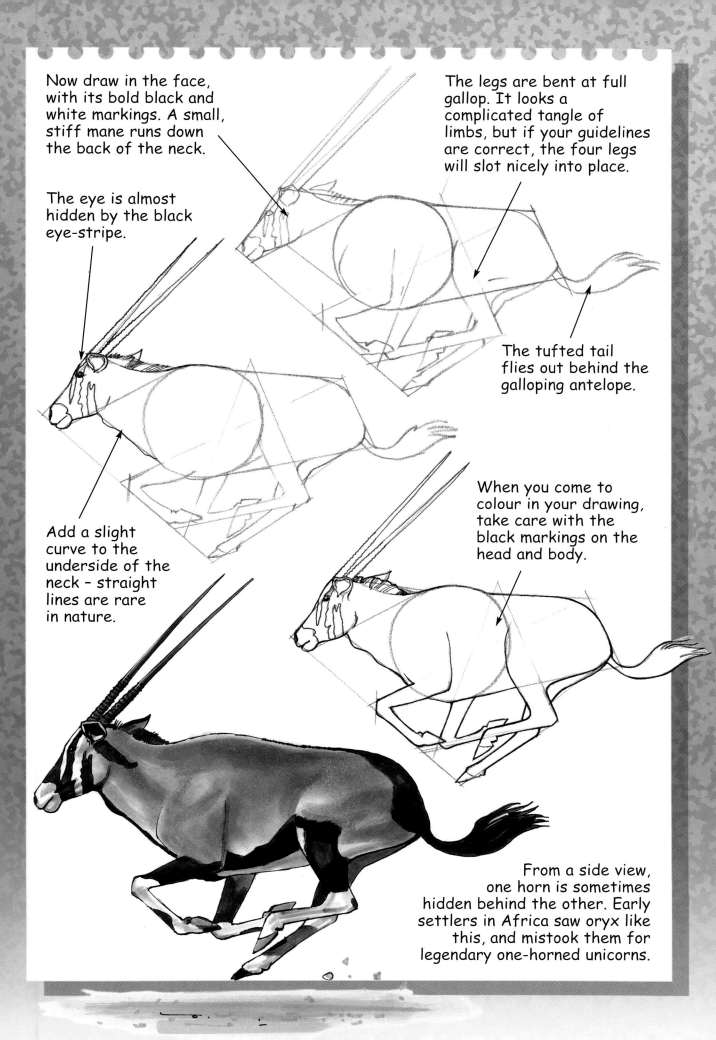

Now draw in the face, with its bold black and white markings. A small, stiff mane runs down the back of the neck.

The eye is almost hidden by the black eye-stripe.

Add a slight curve to the underside of the neck – straight lines are rare in nature.

The legs are bent at full gallop. It looks a complicated tangle of limbs, but if your guidelines are correct, the four legs will slot nicely into place.

The tufted tail flies out behind the galloping antelope.

When you come to colour in your drawing, take care with the black markings on the head and body.

From a side view, one horn is sometimes hidden behind the other. Early settlers in Africa saw oryx like this, and mistook them for legendary one-horned unicorns.

Marabou Stork

This huge African stork has the largest wingspan of any land bird. Clumsy on the ground, it is a master of the air, soaring to great heights to look for food. It hunts all kinds of small animals, and also feeds on carrion.

Start with a large, leaf-like shape for the body and a small circle for the head.

These two lines form guidelines for the long, slender legs. Take care to position them exactly.

Now add the long heavy beak, shaped like a short sword. This is a stabbing weapon, used to kill small prey such as birds, mice and frogs.

Add a curve behind the neck, to give a hunched outline. The long neck is tucked into the body.

Working within your guidelines, draw in the three parts of a leg. Make the upper two sections the same length, and the third (forming the foot) a little shorter.

Draw some wavy lines to mark rows of feathers down the long, broad wings which cover most of the body.

One more line within the framework of the legs gives you the rear leg, which is raised.

The head is bald, like a vulture's.

Storks have no voice. But they are not silent. They make a clapping noise by snapping the upper and lower parts of the beak together. Beak-snapping is part of stork courtship.

A bare pink pouch at the throat is used for display in the breeding season.

The soft fluffy feathers under the wings and tail were once very fashionable for trimming hats and clothes.

Draw the long feet, with their slender toes. The back toe is shorter than the front ones.

Sketch in the long feathers of the wings with soft pencil lines as a guide for your finished drawing.

Marabou Storks gather in great flocks out on the plains. In the dry season they build their nests together in large trees. They also come into towns to seek food on rubbish dumps.

Elephant

The African Elephant is the largest living land mammal. It stands about three times as tall as you are, and weighs as much as seven cars. Even a baby elephant weighs as much as a fully grown man. Asian Elephants are smaller than their African cousins, though they are still huge animals.

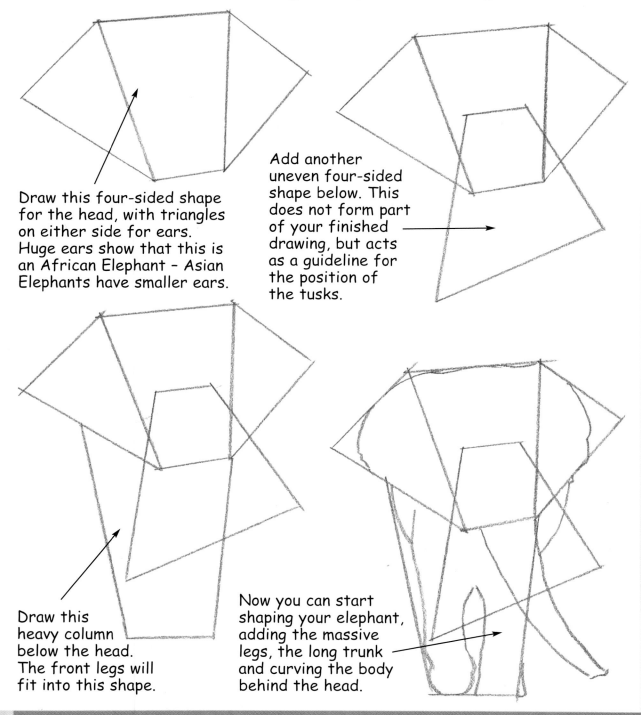

Draw this four-sided shape for the head, with triangles on either side for ears. Huge ears show that this is an African Elephant – Asian Elephants have smaller ears.

Add another uneven four-sided shape below. This does not form part of your finished drawing, but acts as a guideline for the position of the tusks.

Draw this heavy column below the head. The front legs will fit into this shape.

Now you can start shaping your elephant, adding the massive legs, the long trunk and curving the body behind the head.

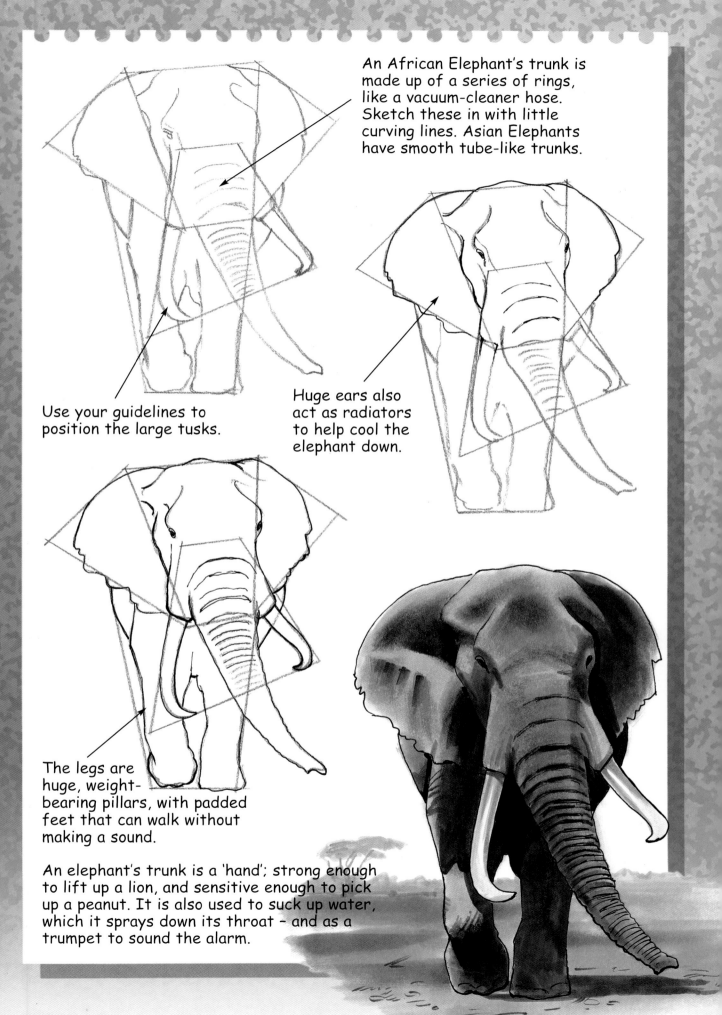

An African Elephant's trunk is made up of a series of rings, like a vacuum-cleaner hose. Sketch these in with little curving lines. Asian Elephants have smooth tube-like trunks.

Use your guidelines to position the large tusks.

Huge ears also act as radiators to help cool the elephant down.

The legs are huge, weight-bearing pillars, with padded feet that can walk without making a sound.

An elephant's trunk is a 'hand'; strong enough to lift up a lion, and sensitive enough to pick up a peanut. It is also used to suck up water, which it sprays down its throat – and as a trumpet to sound the alarm.

Hippo

Its name means 'river horse', but the hippo's nearest relatives are the pig family. It is superbly adapted to a river life. Clumsy on land, that huge body is made for underwater swimming, floating lightly on the surface or walking submerged along the riverbed.

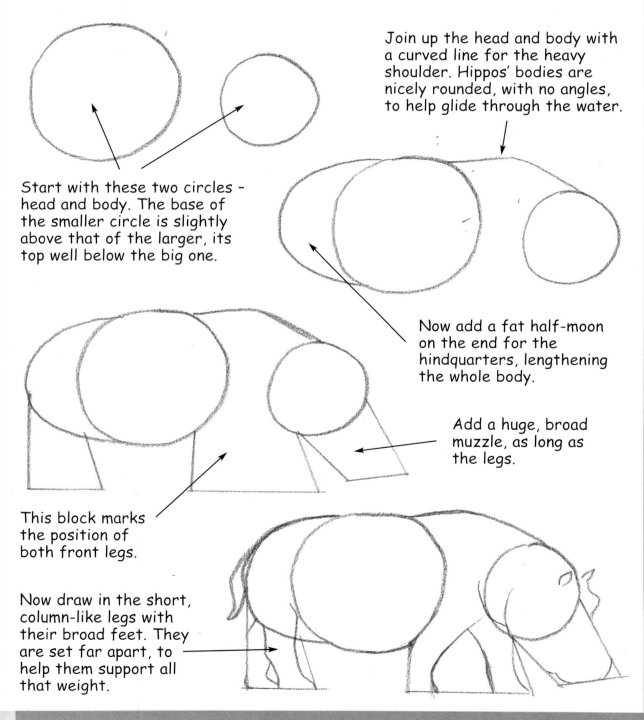

Join up the head and body with a curved line for the heavy shoulder. Hippos' bodies are nicely rounded, with no angles, to help glide through the water.

Start with these two circles – head and body. The base of the smaller circle is slightly above that of the larger, its top well below the big one.

Now add a fat half-moon on the end for the hindquarters, lengthening the whole body.

Add a huge, broad muzzle, as long as the legs.

This block marks the position of both front legs.

Now draw in the short, column-like legs with their broad feet. They are set far apart, to help them support all that weight.

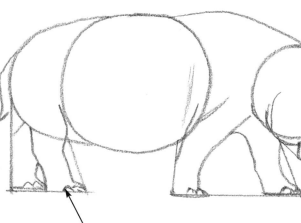

Draw in the face, with small ears and eyes and enormous jaws. Hippos are vegetarians, but those jaws are very effective for fighting other males and for self-defence.

Draw little domes around the eyes. The eyes are raised so they are above water when the rest of the body is submerged.

Each foot ends in four well-developed toes, supporting the weight between them.

The hippo's body is protected by tough skin nearly 5cm thick.

The hippo's jaws can open in an enormous gape, exposing the huge teeth. In defence of their young, hippos have been known to bite small boats in half!

Hippos spend most of the day relaxing in the water. At night they come out to feed, taking well-trodden tracks from the river to their grazing place. The male will attack any trespassers on these private paths.

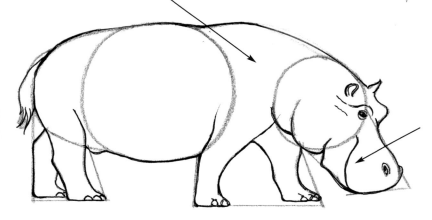

Grizzly Bear

This huge North American bear is bigger than European brown bears. Its name comes from the 'grizzled' or greyish hairs that overlay its brown coat.

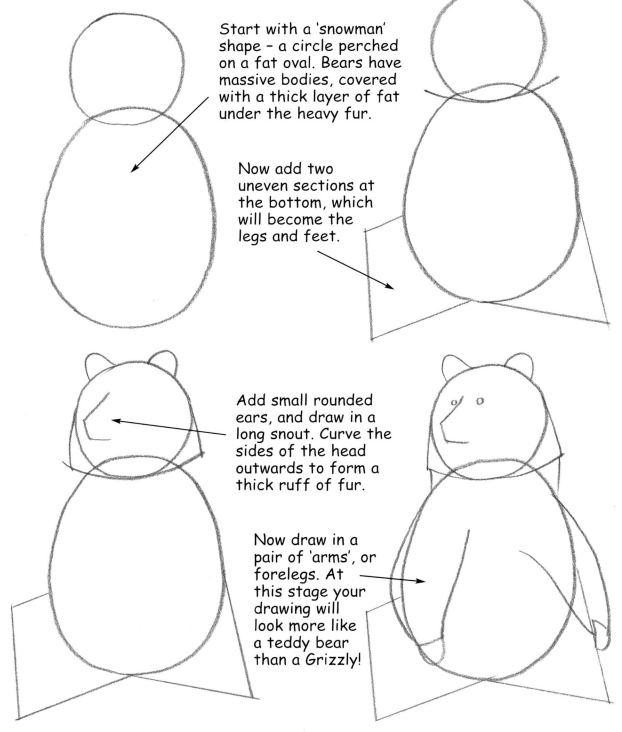

Start with a 'snowman' shape – a circle perched on a fat oval. Bears have massive bodies, covered with a thick layer of fat under the heavy fur.

Now add two uneven sections at the bottom, which will become the legs and feet.

Add small rounded ears, and draw in a long snout. Curve the sides of the head outwards to form a thick ruff of fur.

Now draw in a pair of 'arms', or forelegs. At this stage your drawing will look more like a teddy bear than a Grizzly!

Start developing the face, shaping the nose and mouth. Add a curve above the eyes to make them look more deep-set.

Now you can start sketching in the shaggy fur of the head and neck.

The huge claws, more than 5cm long, are used to dig for roots and burrowing animals like mice and squirrels.

Ink in your outlines, developing the shagginess of the dense coat.

This is a truly powerful animal. It may look clumsy, but it is a master climber and swimmer – and can run as fast as a horse.

Orang-utan

Found only on the south-east Asian islands of Borneo and Sumatra, this giant ape lives in the trees. It feeds on leaves, fruit and flowers, and spends most of its life high above the ground. The world's largest tree-living mammal, it has long, strong arms to pull it through the branches.

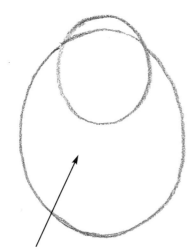

This shape will form the rounded muzzle.

Build this shape with four lines joined to the base of your big oval. It will form the folded limbs.

Start with these two shapes, like short eggs, for the head and body.

Draw the raised arm and hand in three sections. Orangs have unusually long arms, to help them climb.

Divide the face down the centre as a guideline to help you position the eyes and nose.

Add a four-sided shape for one bent back leg, just overlapping the other 'leg' shape.

Draw a hand like your own – only bigger and much more powerful.

Sketch in the coarse, shaggy coat which hangs in 'sleeves' from the arms. Orang-utans have the longest hair of any ape.

Now draw in the details of the face, with its broad nose and deep-set eyes.

The short, bandy legs are used for walking – but, with double-jointed hips, are even more useful as a second pair of 'arms', complete with finger-like toes.

A male orang-utan is four times stronger than an adult man.

At night, orangs build nests in the forks of trees, bending branches to make a secure platform.

'Orang-utan' is a Malay word meaning 'man of the forest'. Apes and humans belong to the same family, and some scientists believe the Orang is our nearest relative.